The Very Basics of Pendulums

Rev. Michael J Dangler

GARANUS
PUBLISHING

Columbus, OH

Published by Garanus Publishing

http://www.lulu.com/garanus

PO Box 3264

Columbus, OH 43210

The Columbus Sanctuary

http://www.columbussanctuary.org/

For more information and related products, please visit

The Magical Druid

http://www.magicaldruid.com/

3165 N. High St.

Columbus, OH 43202

Contents

Introduction: What is a Pendulum?

At its most simple, a pendulum is simply a weight at the end of a line, suspended from a pivot point and allowed to swing freely. This very objective description does not begin to offer an insight into the many ways pendulums are used and the variety of styles you will find as you begin this work.

Pendulums have been used for divination and dowsing (dowsing is a subcategory of divination focused primarily on locating things) for centuries, as well as for healing and energy work. The first mention of a pendulum in use was for scientific purposes in the first century CE in China, where it was used to determine where an earthquake had taken place. Some paranormal investigators use them to follow the trails of ghosts, while dowsers use them to find water or oil hidden in the earth.

Pendulums come in all shapes, sizes, and materials: some are made of crystal, others of metals such as copper, others of wood, and (in a pinch) occasionally a simple metal nut on the end of a piece of kite string. They are both simple to make if you find yourself without your favorite tool, and machined to precision in modern shops.

The most important thing to know about pendulums and their use is that they are flexible, highly portable, and extremely accurate tools that you can take with you wherever you go, and do a wide variety of work with. If you're looking for a great tool to help you or your friends make decisions, locate lost objects, or simply holistically and naturally tune yourself to the world around you, there is no better choice than a pendulum.

We'll start our adventure by learning how to choose the right tool for your work, and then describe some of the varied ways that pendulums can be used to improve your life and the lives of those you care for.

The Real Basics

Divination is an ancient art with many schools. If you are into the fancy words for things, you might call divination by pendulum "**pallomancy**," from the Greek word *pallein* (to sway) and *manteia* (prophecy).

Pendulum use to understand far-off things dates back to the first century CE in ancient China, as we mentioned in the introduction. There, during the Han Dynasty, a Chinese scientist named Zhang Heng set up an apparatus to determine the epicenter of earthquakes by setting a pendulum in an urn at the center of a series of levers. When an earthquake hit, it would shake the pendulum in a particular direction, and a ball would fall out of the urn and into the mouth of a waiting bronze toad sitting in one of the eight compass points, indicating the location of the quake.

Much of the history of pendulums can be traced through scientific discovery and application: pendulums are used to find a right angle with the earth, to keep time accurately, and to measure the rotation of the earth. While being used for science since the first century, the pendulum has also been associated with dowsing and divination for centuries at this point, and these uses may date back as far as the 1500's. Recently, pendulums have been used by police and military personnel to locate weapons and tunnels.

The work of dowsers and diviners revolves around respect for the energies of the land and the folk who use these tools. Those who work with pendulums over time come to understand these tools as an extension of the diviner's senses, a way to help bring out your own natural knowledge of how the cosmos is ordered (and what may be out of order in it).

Choosing a Pendulum

You may have already chosen a pendulum, or you may be seeking one out now. Some believe that the pendulum is the one who does the choosing in most divinatory relationships. One thing is certain, though: when you seek out a pendulum, you should do it in person if at all possible.

Pendulums like to be touched, held, and felt. If you order a pendulum online, you are never quite sure how well that particular pendulum will mesh with your energy, or if it will even respond well.

Your best bet is a spiritual supply shop or local Pagan or New Age store. There, you should find several pendulums, and the shop owner should encourage you to pick them up and get a feel for them.

Pendulums come in a variety of materials, from crystals to metals to wood (we'll get more into this later, when we discuss specific things you can do with pendulums), but the important thing to know about these different materials is that the material is less important than how it feels to you.

Recognizing the pendulum that is "yours" is something you should be able to do, even if you're new to the process of sensing energy or listening to the voice of objects. Here are a couple of simple exercises you can do:

1. Run your hands across the pendulums displayed. You don't have to touch them, just get a general feel. Pick several that appeal to you, and ask to see those specific ones.

2. Hold each pendulum in your hand for a moment. How does it feel, weight-wise? If you're going to be using it indoors, weight is less important than how it feels, but if you'll be using your pendulum outside, consider that a heavier pendulum will help keep the wind from affecting your outcomes. Narrow your choices down a bit.

3. Once you have narrowed down the selection to two or three pendulums, grasp each one in turn by the chain and hold it between your thumb and forefinger. Place your other hand below the pendulum and close your eyes for a moment. Hold still for about 10 seconds, concentrating on the pendulum in your hand.

4. Some pendulums will react strongly to the person holding them, and others less so. If you find one that both feels good in your hand and that seems to react in a way that feels "right" to you, you have the right pendulum there.

Two important things are worth mentioning. First, you're allowed to pick a pendulum that appeals to you visually and that you find simply aesthetically pleasing. Sometimes, that's how the tool calls out to you. Second, you if you can't find one that appeals to you, you don't need to buy one. Sometimes, your pendulum just isn't there.

Once you've got your pendulum, it's time for the real fun to begin!

Cleansing, Charging, and Tuning Your Pendulum

Your new pendulum is almost ready for work immediately, but there's always a bit of work to be done before you can get started. The first thing to do is cleanse, then charge, and then tune your pendulum so that it is completely ready for use, and completely yours.

Cleansing is the first step, and the first thing you should do with your new pendulum. There are several great methods for cleansing, just like with all divination tools, which you can find in a variety of sources. Here's a quick rundown of ways to cleanse your new tool:

- ❖ **Salt and Water:** A very common method is to take salt and add it to water, purifying the water, and using that to cleanse the tool.
- ❖ **Fire and Water:** Another common method is to take incense and water (salted or not) and pass the pendulum through both to cleanse it.
- ❖ **Elemental Cleansing:** This works with all the elements to draw out anything negative and leave the pendulum prepared for charging and tuning (an example of this sort of cleansing is included in the appendix for your convenience).
- ❖ **Sunlight Cleanse:** Leaving the pendulum in the light of the sun from dawn until dusk is a great way to burn off any negative energy.
- ❖ **Earth Burial:** Burying the pendulum at the base of a tree or on a river bank for a night is said to pull any negativity out of the tool and make it ready for charging.

Charging is the next step. Charging is a process that empowers the pendulum with the rhythms of nature, giving the pendulum a greater connection to the earth and the energies that flow through it. Charging is particularly important any time the pendulum has been unused for a long period.

- ❖ **Full Moon Charge:** Probably the most common method of charging a divination tool is to leave it out under the light of the full moon. Some people leave their tool out each full moon, and some leave it out from the new moon until the full moon before its first use.
- ❖ **Rhythmic/Tonal Charge:** Using a drum, bell, singing bowl, or other musical device (perhaps even your bare hands, clapping), create a rhythm or tone that can drive the heartbeat of the earth into the pendulum.
- ❖ **Blessing of the Spirits:** By calling on the spirits you work with, or the general spirits of the realms, you can ask that they help you and charge the pendulum to the rhythms they know well (an example of this sort of charging is included in the appendix for your convenience).
- ❖ **Dancing the Charge:** You can dance and pull the rhythm of the earth into the tool. (This method an also tune the pendulum to your use at the same time, since it combines your rhythm with the earth's.)

Tuning is the final step before you use the pendulum regularly. Where charging was a process that empowered the pendulum with earth energies, tuning will infuse the pendulum with your energy and help it to link to you, giving you more accurate results and a stronger connection. There are several methods of this work as well:

❖ **The Tuning Breath:** This tuning method involves breathing nine breaths over the tool to get it used to your rhythm. Breathe calmly over the tool nine times, and it will get to know you.

❖ **The Inner Tone:** This involves making a vibrating tone as you pour your energy into the tool. Start by holding your hands over the pendulum, and begin to make a sound with your mouth (vowel sounds and "M" sounds work very well for this). Let it vibrate in your chest and flow out from your mouth and through your hands to the tool until you feel it is tuned to you (an example of this sort of charging is included in the appendix for your convenience).

❖ **Pillow Tuning:** Another common divination tool practice is to sleep with the pendulum under your pillow for a night, so that it can get used to your energy at rest.

❖ **Reiki Tuning:** If you are a Reiki practitioner, you can use Reiki or another energy tuning technique you may know.

Many people find that the tuning of a pendulum or other tool has to be done fairly often (some people do it each time they use the tool), while charging is less often (once a month or less), and cleansing is only needed on special occasions. You will eventually find your own schedule, and it's important that you remember that the way you feel about your pendulum is the most important thing.

Holding Your Pendulum

Now that you have a cleansed, charged, and tuned pendulum, it's time to learn how to hold it properly!

You will eventually find the method that works best for you, but most pendulum holders start out by holding the pendulum's line between their thumb and index finger on their primary hand.

Many people will hold the chain or sting around with about 2/3 to 3/4 of the chain left to swing free with the pendulum. Some people merely leave the excess curled up in their remaining fingers on that hand, while others wind the excess string around their index finger. The key is to ensure that the leftover chain does not interfere with the pendulum's movement.

Each time you hold the pendulum, start it from a "neutral" position; that is, don't start it out swinging: let it find its own rhythm without any help.

Now, let's get serious about usage!

Pendulum Divination

One of the first things people want to do with a pendulum is start asking it questions. Pendulums are remarkably versatile when it comes to their ability to help people make decisions, so we're going to go through several examples of how to divine with your pendulum.

Simple Yes/No Divination

Pendulums are somewhat unique in the divination world in that they are able to provide a simple "Yes/No" answer to a question (most of the time: an experienced pendulum user will also tell you that they're great at providing "Maybe's" as well). A pendulum does this in a couple of different ways. We'll start with the basics and work our way up.

Determining is the process of setting a reference for the pendulum's actions. Especially if you are new to this particular pendulum, asking the determining questions is the first thing you should always do. This is one of the most basic (and fun) exercises you can do with your pendulum.

To determine what the pendulum will be telling you, you first have to ask it a simple question.

Take the pendulum up as we learned in the last chapter, and place your other (empty) hand beneath the pendulum palm up. Take a deep breath or two to get centered, and task it with the following:

"Show me 'Yes.'"

And let the pendulum start to work.

The pendulum should begin to move in a certain direction. This could be a back-and-forth motion along a specific axis, or it could be a broad circular motion, clockwise or counterclockwise. The exact direction will depend on both the pendulum and your connection to it.

What it's telling you is what direction means "yes" if you ask it a simple yes/no question.

Some people like to ask their pendulum the opposite question once "yes" is determined: "Show me 'No.'" Most often, this isn't necessary, as "no" can be assumed to be the opposite direction from "yes," but it can be fun to watch it change direction (sometimes quite quickly).

I had mentioned a "maybe" option above: usually, "maybe" is indicated by the pendulum exhibiting a completely counter behavior. As an example, if your "yes" is clockwise and your "no" is counterclockwise, a "maybe" would happen if instead of going around in circles, the pendulum instead went back and forth across an axis.

Similarly, if you had "yes" along a north/south axis and "no" along an east/west axis, "maybe" might be either a NE/SW or NW/SE axis, or a clockwise or counterclockwise spin.

If the pendulum doesn't move at all when you ask your yes/no question, then it's possible that the question simply isn't ready to be answered yet, and you may need to ask again later.

Decision-Making Divination

Building on the "Yes/No" divination, there is a type of divination called "decision-making" divination. This is a process of asking "Yes/No" questions, taking the answers, and building new questions on top of the previous answer.

It is, in many ways, like a reverse version of "20 Questions," where the difference is that you don't actually know the answer until you've asked all the questions.

A simple example might be something like this: Lisa wants to know if she should go out tonight, so she decides to put the question to her pendulum.

First, she asks the pendulum to show her "yes," which both serves to set the stage and to get her into a mindset to ask the questions she needs answers to. Once it has shown her yes, she starts her series of questions.

She asks, "Should I go out tonight?" The pendulum answers that she should.

Building on the question, she asks, "Should I go see a movie?" Here, the pendulum says, "No." "How about the pub?" The pendulum answers "Yes."

"Okay," she says, "Should I call a friend?" The pendulum becomes cryptic and says, "Maybe." Lisa decides that this means she should probably call a specific friend, or else go alone. So she asks, "Should I go with Marty?"

She gets another "No" from the pendulum, and asks, "What about Tammy?" and now she gets a "Yes." So she calls Tammy and they go out.

The example is a bit trite, but it's a good way to describe the process of making a decision based on the pendulum's answers. The same method can be used for determining what job to take, whether to enter a relationship, or even what you might want for breakfast in the morning.

Time Divination

Pendulums can provide not just information on whether or not something will happen, but also when it might occur. Often used in conjunction with other pendulum divination methods, looking at the time it might take for something to occur begins to introduce us to pendulum boards (more on that in the next section).

To determine the time something might happen, you can use a variety of tools: wall calendars with dates marked out, a clock face, or similar items. We're going to use a purpose-built Time Map, though, for this exercise.

The Time Map is a simple representation of time designed to provide a clear idea of when something might happen. In this case, we've based our map off a clock face to determine whether something will happen soon (within the next day) or far in the future (potentially months from now). Here's what our example looks like:

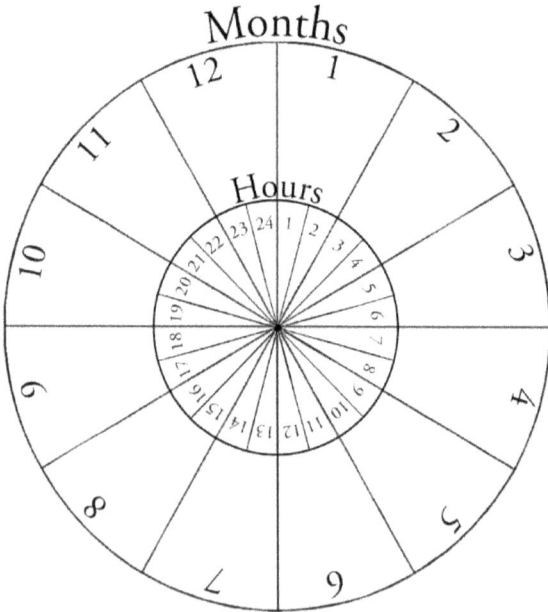

Time Divination Pendulum Board

You can see that there are two circles here, an inner circle divided into 24 (representing hours) and an outer circle divided into 12 (representing months). To keep it simple, we're just going to look at hours and months in this example, but you could make the inner circle represent hours *or* days, and the outer circle represent months *or* years, if you wanted to get something more accurate.

Begin by holding your pendulum over the board, starting centered in the middle of the two circles. Ask the pendulum when something will occur: an example might be, "When is it a good time to start my novel?"

This question might be one that could have an immediate, "Do it now!" sort of response, or a more protracted, "Get everything together first!" sort of response. Novel writing is a serious business and it takes planning to execute well (and a lot of time!).

Let's say that at noon on a Friday, you hold it over the Time Map and it starts to swing back and forth tightly over the "six hours" number. It would suggest a good time for you to write is in the evening, and you should get started tonight. If it were over the "20 hours" number, maybe you're a morning writer and would be best served writing early.

If you get a broader swing, though, and it goes out over the "six months" range, then you might want to evaluate the amount of planning you've already done and maybe do a bit more.

Note about Time Divination: Divination, in general, is concerned with what has already happened, and where you are today. If you change things in your life and work toward shortening that time (say, in our example, you pour yourself into preparing to write that novel after getting a "six months" answer: you do outlines, imagine characters, and maybe sketch out a map of a fantastic world for your setting), then you can ask again to see if circumstances have changed and your timeline has moved up or back (in this example, if it moves back, then maybe you're headed the wrong way down the novel's path, and perhaps that's not the story you should be telling).

Dowsing Boards, Charts, and Pendulum Tools

Pendulum or dowsing boards are a great way to simplify your work, and make it easier for you to know what's going on when you ask a question. The Time Divination board is one example of a board that you might use regularly to examine the effects of time on your divination, but there are plenty of others that you might look at using as well.

Perhaps the most common style of pendulum board is the simple "Yes/No" board. These can be elaborate designs, or they can be very simple boards sketched out on paper and held in the palm of your hand.

A "Yes/No" board tends to have as few as three, and as many as eight, different indicators on them: usually, there is at least a position (though sometimes two each) for "Yes," "No," and "Maybe" (where there are two "Yes/No" illustrations, there's often four "Maybe's").

A simple "Yes/No" board we provide in our shop looks like this, and is burned onto wood about one and a half inches across, with a symbol for the wild god in the center of the disc:

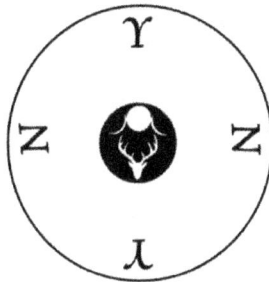

This board just gives you two options: the "Yes" or "No" directions, and is great for a quick check on the temperature of a decision.

A more elaborate board might look like this, with eight indicators, adding in uncertainty with a pair of "Maybe" axes:

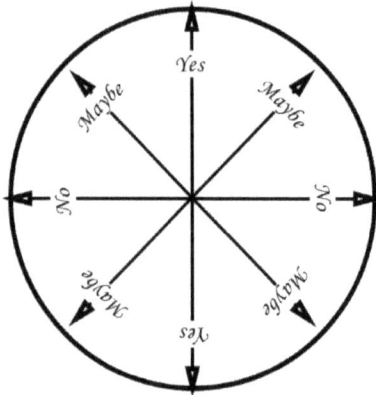

Beyond "Yes/No" boards, one of the other most common types of pendulum tools is an alphabet board. These come in many different configurations, often being round, but also often being half-circles, as pictured here:

This arrangement allows you to begin with your pendulum steady in the middle, and (much like a spirit board) ask the pendulum to spell out what you need to know.

A particularly useful mechanism you can use is, if you are familiar with a magical alphabet, you can take this concept and expand it into that for a bit of extra "oomph." Here's the same concept, with the elder futhark replacing the alphabet:

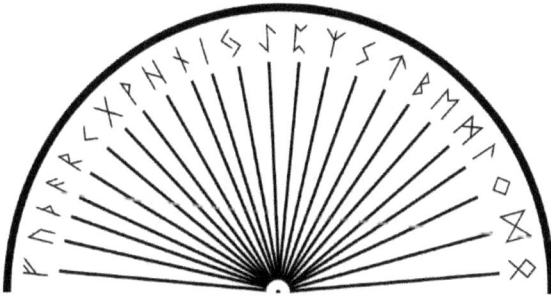

Most people using pendulums on a board like this will use it to obtain the first letter of something, or initials of a person's name.

Pendulum Boards for Spell-Work

Pendulum boards can be excellent for helping you work magic, simply by providing you with a deeper knowledge of the things that affect a spell.

Examples of this might include creating pendulum boards to help you determine what kind of offerings to make, what spirits you should call on, or what color of candle to use.

For deciding which color of candle to use, an easy method is to find a simple color wheel and use that to provide you with guidance.

If you are interested in which herb you should use for a spell, you might use an alphabet board like in the previous section to spell out the name of a spirit, or you might have it give you the first letter of an herb. You could even use the time divination board in the previous section to help you determine when might be a good time to do the work.

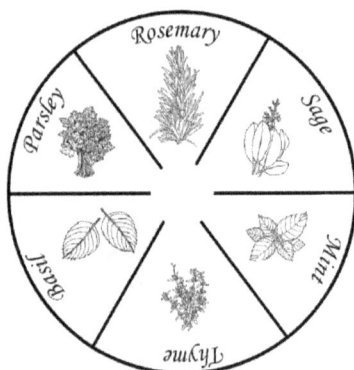

Of course, with that particular set of herbs, you may also find this pendulum board particularly good for cooking a chicken, as well.

You can also use boards to help you determine what sorts of associations might be best for your particular kind of spell. If you were working to create a spell to study better, you could ask the pendulum what element you should work with to achieve that aim on a board like this one:

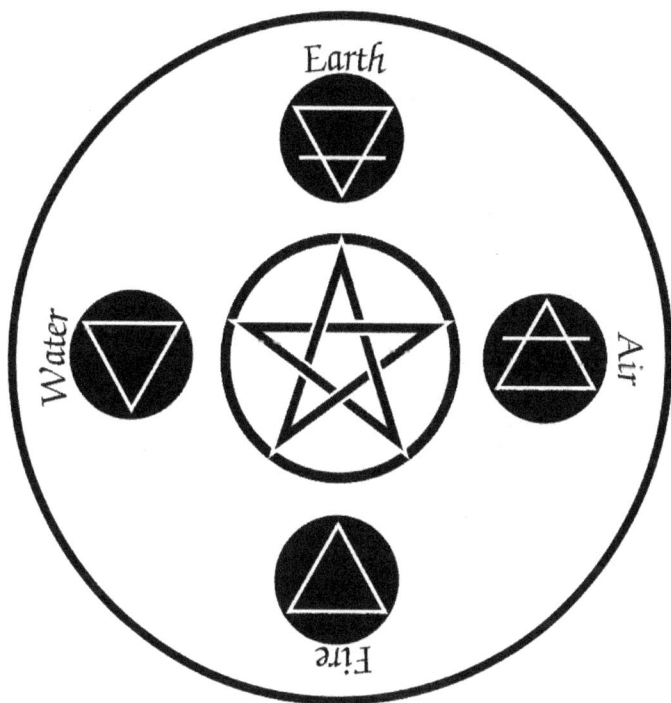

Here, the pendulum should swing over or in the direction of the element to be worked with in your particular kind of spell. The center (pentacle) is, of course, Spirit.

A more complicated board might be this one, which comes from old grimoires: here (in an image from the second book of the Lemegaton), you see the various angels associated with various directions, their names inscribed on the directions. At the center, you have a time signifier (seasons), as well as the elements (earth, air, fire, water) and the Aristotelian properties of those elements (dry, cold, moist, hot).

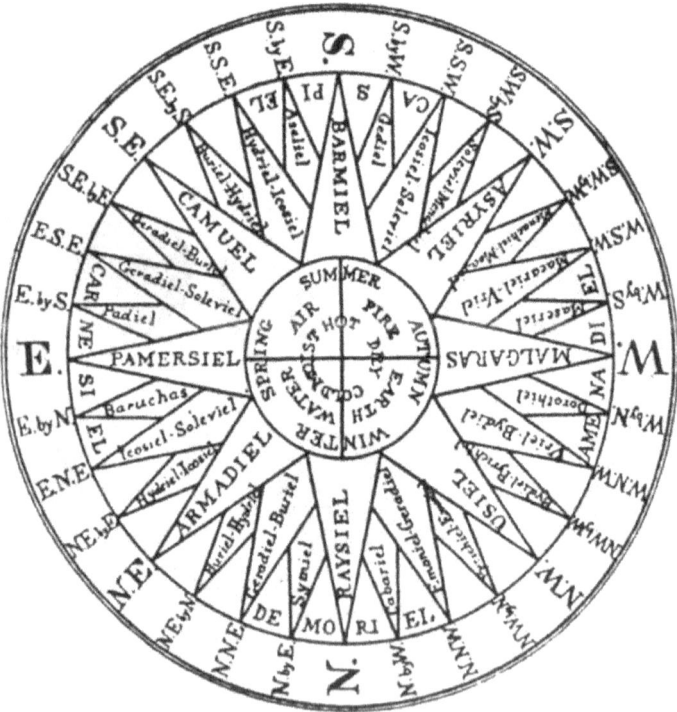

This particular illustration from the Lemegaton is one of the few particularly useful seals when it comes to pendulum divination, but others can be used as well, in similar ways.

Of course, you can make specific boards based on your spirituality and needs. This board was designed specifically as a Druidry board, with the Nine Virtues laid out around the center, and a simple "Yes/No/Maybe" dividing them up.

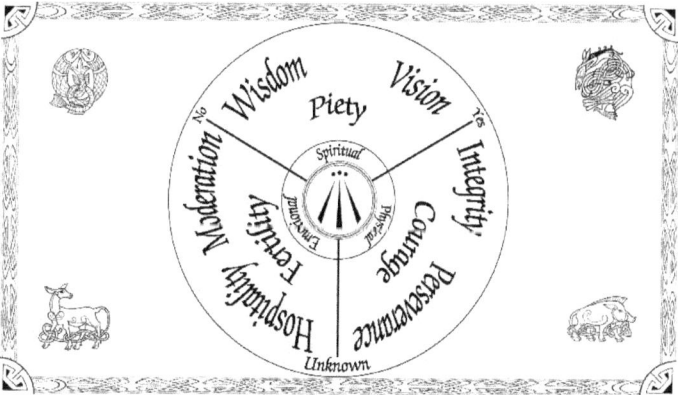

Intensity Charts

A common reason for using a pendulum is to determine the intensity of a thing. These can be used in two ways: 1) to lead you to the strongest intensity of a thing, or 2) to help you understand the change in intensity over time.

To create an intensity chart, you simply need a scale where one side is the lowest, and one side is the highest. A scale of 1 to 10 is fairly common for this, though any number range will do.

Linear Intensity Chart

①②③④⑤⑥⑦⑧⑨⑩

Less Intense   *More Intense*

For a linear intensity chart, like above, set your pendulum at neutral on the far left, and the more intense something is, the further toward 10 it will swing. This can show you how far something is from you, or how concentrated it is.

You can also make an intensity chart like the alphabet boards. Start your neutral at the center and radiate out toward the intensity. This can also give you gradations of intensity (so, a small swing toward 1 might register as a half, etc.)

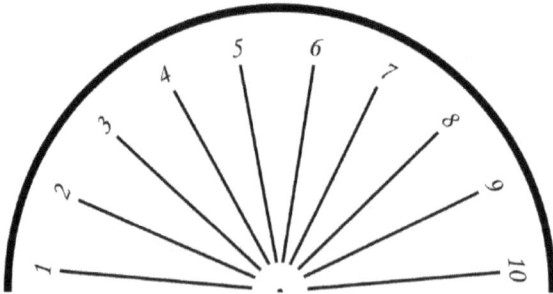

You can also combine time and intensity to understand how much something has affected a person in the past, present, or future. If you want to know about what concerns are strongest for a person, devising a board that deals with time and intensity might be helpful. Here is an example board:

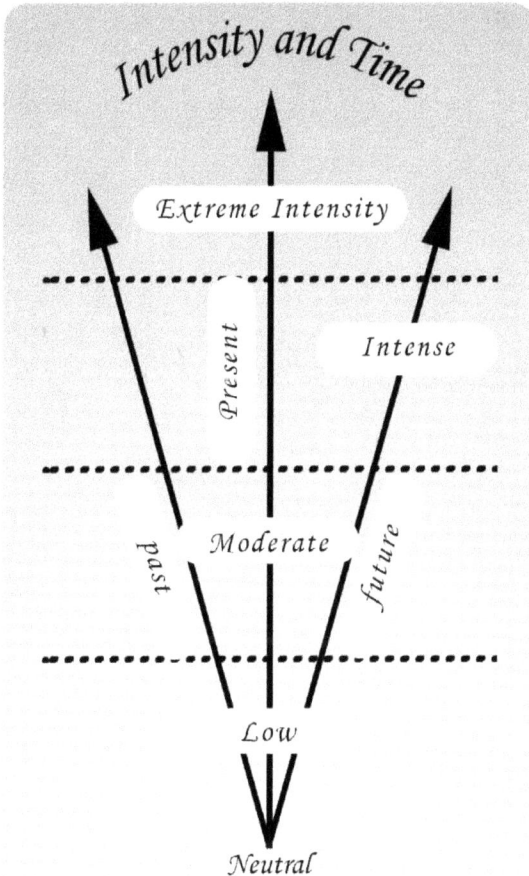

Be creative in your use of pendulum boards: make your own, and let the pendulum help you as you do. After all, you're building a common language between yourself and the pendulum: it's only fair that the pendulum should get to help as well. Let it show you what it wants to show you, and use that to draw out the pendulum.

Dowsing: Seeking For Yourself and Others

Dowsing is the process of discovering the unknown, typically and specifically things that are lost or covered, or whose direction is unclear. We've discussed some aspects of dowsing with a pendulum before (particularly, intensity charts), but we're going to look more specifically at practical applications now: everything from finding water or lost items to understanding the directions decisions might take you.

Water Witching

Dowsing has long been associated specifically with seeking water: you may have seen old movies or cartoons where a person will walk around with a forked stick until it dips toward the earth, and there they find water. This is the "Hollywood" version of dowsing, but it's not far from the truth. We'll be discussing something very similar, but with a pendulum instead of the traditional dowsing rod.

We know certain things about water: it flows downhill, it collects, and there are unseen places where it flows beneath the land. Additionally, places where the water breaks through are often sacred and powerful, so it stands to reason that we can detect them.

We're going to use all this information, plus the pendulum, to seek out and locate water, and also to tell if it's safe for the uses we have for it.

Hazel is a traditional wood for witching or water, so you might consider seeking a pendulum made from this wood if this is something you would like to seek deeply (and, since many of the techniques here can also be used for finding metals underground, it's worth noting that rowan, the mountain ash, is a tree traditionally associated with that activity).

Finding the Water

Begin with observation, always: look at the surroundings and apply what you know about the land, if anything, to give you a place to start. Form your intention clearly in your mind as you do this, and prepare yourself mentally for the search.

Are you looking for a place to sink a well? Are you looking for a natural spring? Are you looking for a space to build your house and want it away from the water? Knowing what you seek is the first step in finding it.

Once you've set your intention into your mind, bring out your pendulum. An intensity chart can help start you off in the right direction, if you aren't sure which way to begin: ask the pendulum to tell you where the water is most likely to be.

Once you've found your neutral, and have a direction to go in, you should do a quick visualization exercise. Close your eyes and let the landscape before you become transparent in your mind, and seek the water below you: look for it, and imagine where the waters are likely to flow from and to in this direction. Get a good idea of where you might need to go from that.

Open your eyes again, once you have that "map" in your head, and begin to walk in the direction you feel most pulled toward.

Watch the pendulum closely. You want to see how it reacts to your surroundings, and it will help guide you on your way. This might be through a simple "Yes/No" reading when you come to a decision point about which way to go, or it might be through a clear change in behavior when you get close to a water source (many people report that a pendulum near a water source will "go wild" and spin in an impressive circle; others say that it changes direction, either going from back-and-forth to side-to-side, or vice versa). Either way, let the pendulum guide you on the path.

Once you feel like you have reached the water source you are seeking, re-set the pendulum to "neutral" and ask it if this is the place that best fits the idea you had in your mind when you started. Do a check against the landscape you visualized when you started as well: does this feel like the proper place?

If you're looking for water that is underground (for instance, a place to sink a well), you might pull out an intensity chart to find out how close the water is to the surface, or a number chart to tell you how many feet you'll have to drill to reach it (this might take some knowledge of the water table: if you know the water table is near the top, you can use "number of feet" on a scale of 1-10; if the water table is deep, you might need to multiply your scale by 10 or more to get an accurate reading).

You can also check to find the flow rate of the water you've found with your pendulum: an intensity chart is great for this as well: the more intense the reading, the greater the flow.

Then comes the fun part: sink your well and see if you were right!

Is It Potable?

While we hardly offer medical advice, you can do a quick check on water that you have witched to see if it is adequate to your needs.

If you're in a situation where you want to know the quality of the water really quickly (such as if you're buying land and want to decide if it's worth the investment to hire someone to come in and professionally test it, or you're out hiking and need a quick check), you can check it with your pendulum.

If you have an intensity board with you, or you want to make one, you can ask on a scale of 1-10 how safe the water is to drink, and make an informed decision from that.

Another option is to check for specific contaminants you might want to be aware of: when buying an old house, ask your pendulum if there is lead in the pipes, or rust, or any other contaminant you might be concerned about.

Of course, you can always do a simple "Yes/No" question to get a really quick gut-check on whether it's safe.

Remember that water sources change in their level of cleanliness, even when it's the same body of water, just further downstream. Check multiple points to see how things are, and choose the cleanest one to drink from.

This process involves only a first check: if you can, have water tested professionally before drinking it, or put it through a purifier if you're hiking. Relying on a carbon filter doesn't make your dowsing any less effective, but it does make you less likely to get the runs.

Locating the Lost

Finding lost items is both fun and occasionally profitable, but it's also a basic skill that any dowser should have at his or her command.

Much like locating water, finding lost items often involves looking for things that might have been misplaced, or might have been intentionally moved. I've known people to dowse for their keys, lost change, treasure, and even cats (which are, of course, the hardest things ever to dowse for).

Much like the process for water witching, you might want to start with what you know about where the object might have been last, or (in the case of a pet) which direction it was last seen going. From there, you can use an intensity chart to find out which direction you should begin your search in, or, if you don't know enough at all to start there, you can use a compass board or a map (see the next two sections on this).

Ask your pendulum to provide two specific kinds of behaviors when trying to locate lost items:

1) Show direction and changes clearly.
2) Show an obvious change when you reach the object.

Directions can be shown by a swing in the right direction, or they can be shown by a "Yes/No" indication when you get to a decision point and you need to change direction. But the indication should always be clear. If you find yourself at a point where it has become unclear, give the pendulum a few moments to re-center itself and tell you where to go again.

Many people like their pendulum to begin to swing around in broad circles when they get close to the item that was lost. The closer you come, the broader the circle should be.

Occasionally, as you get closer to a thing that is particularly distant or far off, you might have to re-set and re-calibrate the pendulum: because the chain is only so long, you might end up being "closer than you were" but not "close enough to see the thing you seek." If this happens, and your pendulum is going wild but you can't see what you were looking for, re-set the pendulum to neutral and start again. Being a longer distance than expected can cause you to have to re-calibrate the pendulum a few times before you finally find the item.

PSI-Tracks

Discovered by Göte Andersson[1], psi-tracks are the measurable track of a directed thought. You can think of them as "lines of thought" that connect a person to an object, often through an aura reading or similar psychic phenomena (we'll discuss auras later).

Psi-tracks can be used to follow the path of an item, and to locate it. Starting with the person, you read the direction and distance of the object from them.

---

[1] See http://www.hessdalen.org/sse/program/psi-track.pdf for more information on psi-tracks

Begin by having the person who has lost the item concentrate on it. They should visualize the item if they can, and remember their emotional connection to it. Once they've done this, you can tune your pendulum into that "vibe" that they put out, and you can use the person as your "neutral," and work around them to find out which direction the line goes out from them.

If the thing was lost in a certain place, or if it was last seen in a certain place, you can sometimes establish the psi-tracks from that place specifically: it makes a good starting point.

Let the pendulum be your guide here, as it is with so many other techniques: watch it move and show you which direction the thing went.

Psi-tracks begin to degrade after about an hour, it seems, so they become harder and harder to locate as time goes by. Passion and emotion can strengthen the connection, however, and can keep a psi-track active longer. Psi-tracks are particularly useful for tracking things (such as pets and children) who move on their own in odd patterns.

Compasses

The simple compass rose is an excellent indicator of which direction to go to find things. After all, they already look like pendulum boards:

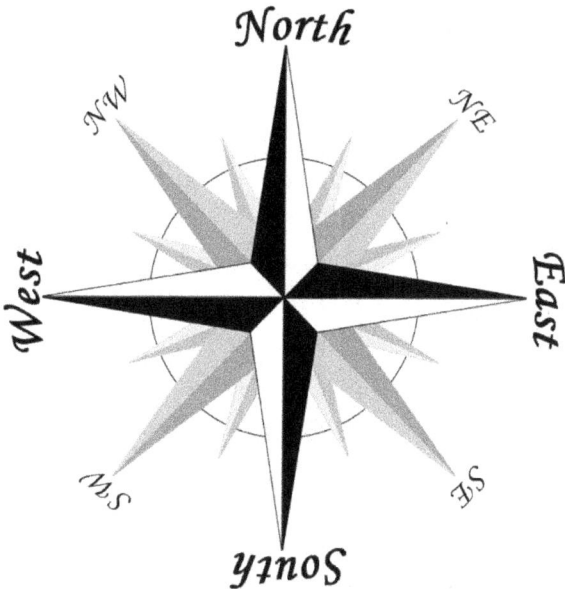

Here, your neutral is obviously at the center, and you can stand in a single place and determine which direction you wish to go. The caveat with compasses is that it is important that you set your compass to either true or magnetic north so that when you begin looking, you know which direction corresponds with an actual orienteering compass.

Setting the orientation with "true" or "magnetic" north becomes even more important when we start to look at pendulums and maps, if used in conjunction with the compass as a dowsing board.

Pendulums and Maps

Maps are an old dowser's best friend: while the map is not the territory, and there are distinct differences between the two, the map can act as an overlay and an easy indicator of what might be where.

Most map dowsing is done in conjunction with the compass. Just as you did with the compass before, align the map with either "true" or "magnetic" north (and note the legend on the map to help you determine this orientation). The reason you want to line these up is that magnetic north can be off quite a bit from true north, and if you mix up the two (most maps are aligned to true north, and all analog compasses point to magnetic north). Where I live, it's 7° (or almost 2% of a circle) of a difference.

There are several good methods for using a pendulum and a map, but I'm going to cover two specific ones: grids and psi-tracks.

Dowsing With Map Grids

One of the single most popular ways to use a map to dowse is by dividing the map into a grid, and then running a simple "Is it here: Yes or No?" question over each grid square. This is a quick and efficient way to narrow your search pattern on the ground.

You can also use an intensity board with the map grid, asking for each grid, "How intense is the feeling here?"

As you visit each grid square, focus on it and then write the number from the intensity board in the gird. You can search the grid spaces with the highest number first, that way, which can speed up the time considerably if you get a number of "maybe" answers from the simple "Yes/No" question.

Once you have settled on a square to search first, you can subdivide it further to make a new grid, and focus the search even better. This works particularly well for very small items, or groups of items that might have been scattered about.

You can, in fact, subdivide grids indefinitely, if you have enough detail to make it worth your while.

Maps and PSI-Tracks

Maps are an ideal way to follow psi-tracks as well: you can ask a person to concentrate on the item that they are seeking, and from there mark out the path that the item has taken from where they last saw it.

Start with the point where it was last seen, or (if that is unknown) use the grid option from the previous section to find a likely starting point. From there, having the person continue their concentration on the thing to be discovered, let the pendulum lead you across the map.

It is important to mark out the path that is taken, and then to follow it in the real world: especially in the case of animals or children who might be scared, their psychic impression might lead you astray if you only go to the end of the path.

The reason for this is that when a child or animal is scared, it may be so focused on a desire to go somewhere that its tracks go from the place it is actually located to the place it desires to be: a cold child might think of his mother, so the psi-tracks might lead to the house, or a dog might dream of a warm fire the night before when out hunting, and so its psi-tracks might lead back to a campsite.

Objects can have similar issues, particularly stolen objects that are lost after they are stolen: a thief might take a wallet out of a purse he has stolen and discard the purse but keep the wallet. If the purse remains missing you might lose evidence that could help convict the thief, should you catch him.

Alternatively, something could be lost along the way of a walk, and the person may think they had it longer than they did. If you go to the end of their walk, rather than re-tracing it, you may not find the object at all.

Even though things often end up at the end of the track, it is best to search the entire length of the track to avoid this particular pitfall.

Ley Lines and Power Centers

Have you ever stood in a place that is filled with power, where energy seems to pool and surge around you? It is entirely possible that you were standing in a power center.

Stonehenge, Woodhenge, and Avebury are some of the great western power centers, and serves as an excellent example. Every continent has numerous power centers, places where energy gathers and brightens the earth. Some are natural, some are man-made, and some are clearly a combination of the two (like the henges mentioned above).

Between each power center are what are called "ley lines." The term was coined in 1921 by Alfred Watkins (after an Anglo-Saxon word for cleared strips of land): each power center, he theorized, had lines that connected it to other power centers, and this helped to align them with one another.

Many people have since come to the understanding that ley lines provide connections to the spirits as well: they are said to be the pathways that the faeries travel as they change homes at Beltaine and Samhain, and ancient ceremonial processional ways.

Modern ley lines are occasionally created, as well: I know of one that is anchored on a farm in Michigan, and the anchor was set there recently (within a year of this writing). Just as sacred spaces aren't always permanent fixtures upon the land, so too with ley lines.

One exciting pastime you might engage in is the location of ley lines and power centers. A "power center" is best described as where two ley lines cross, drawing the earth energies to a specific place. Where three or more ley lines cross, you will find a power nexus. Stonehenge, the Great Pyramid of Giza, and the Pyramid of the Sun at Teotihuacan are all examples of such nexuses.

It is always easiest to begin at a sacred site: check your local historical society for one near you, or open a map and find the headwaters of your local river, or a spring.

From there, begin as you often do by finding a neutral. Just as with water witching, you might find it useful to visualize the sacredness of the space you are in: open your mind to the magic of the area, and see the power of the earth as it arises or collects. It might appear as a white light, or a soft glow, or even as shining water rolling around the space.

Now, let you pendulum help you choose a direction. Ask it to show you one of the ley lines that stretches out from this power center, and then begin to follow it. You might be surprised where it may lead you.

Ley lines tend to move in straight lines between power centers. Usually, when you come to a place where the ley line ends (there is often an anchor point there, something to which the ley line is "affixed" in an energetic sense), you will likely be able to pick up another.

If you watch the line on the cross-quarter festivals (that is, the old festivals between the solstices and equinoxes), you may find yourself viewing spirits as they travel from home to home. Of course, remember what happens to people who spy on the fae as well.

So, what are we seeing here? The ley lines provide a method of transferring the holy power of the earth from one place to another, and holy places sit upon their junctions to both produce and absorb that energy. Following a ley line can bring you into contact with the faery folk, as well as show you sacred places you might not normally see if you just stayed "on the beaten path."

Follow a ley line and you never know what kind of interesting power centers you might come across. It's well worth an adventure!

The Ghost Path

One of the more interesting things to do with your pendulum is to follow the path of a ghost as it moves through a space. Many ghost-hunters use a method like this to re-create the steps a ghost might take in the afterlife, and you can use it as well. It's quite similar to finding and following a ley line, but far less straight.

Go to the source of a haunting, or a reported haunting, and set your pendulum to neutral. As with the ley lines, let the pendulum give you direction.

Follow the path of the ghost wherever it may lead to possibly have an encounter, or to discover the cause of the haunting.

Just as ley lines are often "anchored" to some physical object, so too are some ghost paths. You can use this method to locate haunted objects, or the place where a haunting started, and with that information, you can do what is necessary to end the haunting, as well, if it is malicious.

Healing and Energy Work

Healing and energy work are two very common practices for pendulum users, and both are simple to understand, but difficult to master. We will cover healing, chakras, sensing energy, and reading auras in this section.

Healing with Pendulums

Pendulums are excellent tools for healing: many people find the act of healing another person to be draining or exhausting, and a pendulum does a great job in helping to mitigate that energy drain.

Pendulums can also point directly at the cause of a problem, and help you determine the best way to go about healing that problem. Finally, they are great (particularly in conjunction with an intensity board) at telling you how severe the issue is, which is particularly helpful on pets and things that cannot speak and give you direct feedback on what is wrong.

Begin by asking permission of the affected person to do healing work. This is always good practice, and it gets both of you into the mindset to heal: it gets you ready to give energy, and gets them ready to receive it.

If you are not sure where the ailment resides in their body, you can ask the pendulum to indicate where the problem is. You can also do this for what we call "maintenance healing," where you are working to discover issues before they manifest, or offer healing to a person who isn't sure what is wrong (they may say, "I just feel tired all the time," or "I'm not sure what's going on").

Once you know where the ailment resides, you can start to work on it. There are a couple of methods to try:

1) **Winding the Illness Down:** This is a very simple healing, where you hold the pendulum over the ailing part of the person and let the pendulum spin in its natural direction. This is the direction of increasing illness. Concentrate on and visualize a reduction in the illness, and watch the pendulum begin to spin slower in that direction until it stops or begins to spin in the other direction. Let the pendulum continue until you feel that the illness has "wound down."

2) **Stone Healing:** You can take a stone of a particular property (for instance, red jasper for protection, or rose quartz for heart ailments) and set it on the appropriate body part. Then, hold the pendulum over the stone and push the needed energies into the person as the pendulum swings.

3) **Color Healing:** Similar to stone healing (and related to the chakra alignment in the next section), you can choose a color that has benefits for the ailment a person has. Again, place a swatch of the color on the person and direct the color waves into them with the pendulum.

4) **Candle Healing:** Related to color healing, you can take a candle of a particular color, light it, and then hold the pendulum over it to absorb the energy of the candle. Then, take it to the person and hold it over the afflicted area, and let the warmth of the flame and the healing color flow to the person. This is a great way to store healing energy in your pendulum during a healing ritual, and then take it to the person who needs it later.

These are four very simple ways to heal with your pendulum. Spend some time trying them on yourself, or on others who you know need some healing.

Chakra Alignment with Pendulums

One of the key processes associated with pendulums is the alignment of chakras. Chakras are energy points within the human body, aligned and often described as either "open" or "closed."

The word "chakra" means "wheel," and you can think of each chakra as a place where *nadiis* (or "energy channels" meet. You can also think of chakras as power centers connected by the ley line that is your spine.

As we go through life, our chakras come into and go out of balance. Sometimes, they close up, and sometimes they open wide. A key to chakra health is this word: "Balance."

When your chakras are in balance, you are free to do as you will in the world. When they are not, or when they are blocked, you may have problems associated with the chakra in question.

Problems with love tend to relate to the heart chakra, while people who are shouted at by their boss or a loved one might develop an issue with the throat chakra.

If working on other people, it is often best to have them lie down, though you can also have them stand up for this working. If you're working on yourself, sometimes it's easier to use a pendulum board instead, with each of the chakras laid out in a line (see illustration in this section).

Start by placing the pendulum over the root chakra. The natural motion should be for the pendulum to spin in a clockwise manner over the chakra center. If your pendulum does not swing, then the chakra is blocked. If it swings slowly, it is partially blocked. If it swings in a counterclockwise manner, then the chakra is out of alignment.

So, what do we do in each case? The aim is to get the chakra re-opened and flowing correctly.

- **Blocked:** When a chakra is blocked, it often seems like there is no movement on a particular front. A heart chakra that is blocked might mean that the person is not feeling love on an emotional level. Concentrate on getting the wheel to turn again. It might take more than one session.
- **Partially Blocked:** When a chakra is partially blocked, a person tends to feel out-of-sorts on that front. A partially blocked root chakra might indicate issues with fertility that can be corrected fairly easily. Here, you should be able to re-set the chakra and open the "door" more, and set the wheel spinning right just through concentration and focus. When the pendulum is swinging at a good rate in a clockwise manner, the blockage is gone.
- **Out of Alignment:** When a chakra is out of alignment, things are often going very wrong on the thing the chakra in question has influence over. An out of alignment third eye chakra might mean that the person is having nightmares or bad dreams. To set this right, you need to reduce the issue just like "winding down" the illness in the last section. Set it right and get it going in a clockwise direction again.

The Seven Chakras

Sahasrara - Crown
Top of the Head

Ajna - Third Eye
Center of Forehead

Vishuddha - Throat
Center of Throat

Anahata - Heart
Center of Chest

Manipura - Solar Plexus
Above the Navel

Svadhishthana - Sacral
Lower Abdomen

Muladhara - Root
Base of the Spine

Once you've set the root chakra to be open (or if it's blocked and you can't reopen it just this moment), move up to the next chakra. Repeat as needed to get through all the chakras.

Any time you do an alignment, you should always do all seven chakras: leaving someone half-aligned is leaving them out-of-alignment. Always start at the bottom and work your way up, too: energy mostly flows from bottom to top through the chakras, so it's best to go with the flow here.

Reading an Aura

An aura is an energetic field that surrounds the body: humans, animals, plants, and even stones have auras. These fields can tell us a lot about a person, or about what is going on in their life.

The first step in aura work is to find the barrier of the aura. Some people have large, expansive auras, and some people have very small, restrictive auras. Step back about ten paces with the pendulum in its neutral position, and then approach them slowly. The pendulum will react when it touches their aura.

This is your starting point for all aura work: the place where the aura's furthest extent reaches to. Auras are not always perfect spheres, but you can generally assume that the place you first encounter the aura is a good place to start.

To do a simple scan of a person's aura, you can hold the pendulum at the boundary of their aura at its neutral position, and then move it around the body slowly. When the pendulum moves out of neutral, you've come across a variation in the aura. Positive variations tend to push out from the body, and negative variations tend to bring the aura in closer to the body.

Your "Yes/No" position on the pendulum should tell you which direction to go: if you see a "yes," you have probably found a positive variation; a "no" means a negative one. Push or pull the pendulum until you determine the new edge, and make a note of where it was. I usually number these variations, and have a brief description of where I found it for later reference, because we'll come back to them.

Once you've "mapped" the aura to some extent, it's time to get to work on it. Start with the first negative variation, and ask the person to lie down. Holding your pendulum over their feet, ask the pendulum where the problem is. Move the pendulum up their body until the pendulum indicates the issue, and then seek to clear it with the pendulum.

Then, move on to the next issue, again starting at the feet, and seeking the root cause of the issue.

Do this until all the issues are resolved, and you will have a person with a cleansed and happy aura on your hands!

Appendix: Rituals

These three rituals, a cleansing, a charging, and a tuning, are designed to work together. You can do them separately, but when you are just starting with a new tool, it is wise to do them all at once.

Most people find that they need to tune their tool most often (some do it each time they use it), charge it slightly less often (some do it as often as monthly), and cleanse only when needed. You will settle into a rhythm of your own over time, but it's recommended that if you don't use your tool for a long period of time, that you go through all three steps again.

The setup is the same for all three rituals; in each direction, place the following items:

❖ North: A small container of salt
❖ East: An unlit stick of incense
❖ South: A lit candle
❖ West: A vessel of water
❖ Center: A flat representation of "Spirit" that speaks to you

Once you are set up, you are ready for any of these rituals.

A Simple Elemental Cleansing

Take up your pendulum and place it in the center of your altar, atop the representation of Spirit. To cleanse your pendulum, we will be combining the elements to bring the pendulum into harmony with the cosmos, and cleanse it of all negativity.

Begin with a simple prayer:

> **I call out to the Elements:**
> **To Earth and Air,**
> **To Fire and Water,**
> **And to the Spirit that animates all.**

> **Today, I cleanse a tool for cunning work:**
> **I ask your blessing on this path.**

Take up the container of salt, and begin a prayer to the Earth Power:

> **I call to the powers of the Earth:**
> **The spirits who calm and cool the land,**
> **This salt is your work,**
> **Cleansing with stillness and dark.**

Take up the vessel of water, and begin a prayer to the Water Power:

I call to the powers of the Waters:
The spirits of spray and depth,
This water is your work,
Cleansing with wave and surf.

Take up the candle, and begin a prayer to the Fire Power:

I call to the powers of Fire:
The spirits that dance and spin,
This fire is your work,
Cleansing with passion and joy.

Take up the stick of incense, and begin a prayer to the Air Power:

I call to the powers of Air:
The spirits that fly and glide,
This incense is your work,
Cleansing with focus and magic.

Now, take the incense and the salt in your hands, and pour the salt into the water and light the stick of incense from the candle, saying:

The Earth fills the Water,
The Fire brightens the Air,
Together they mix and mingle:
And brighten my Spirit!

Set both the lit incense into its holder and the vessel of salted water back down. Take up your pendulum, bathing it in the water and passing it through the incense smoke three times each as you pray over it:

> In the Waters that birthed the sun, I cleanse you.
> In the Fire that brightens the way, I cleanse you.
> In the Waters that birthed the sun, I cleanse you.
> In the Fire that brightens the way, I cleanse you.
> In the Waters that birthed the sun, I cleanse you.
> In the Fire that brightens the way, I cleanse you.

Place the pendulum back upon the symbol of spirit, and pray:

> Warmed by Fire, Purified by Air,
> Cleansed by Water, Grounded in Earth,
> With a Spirit that dances and sings:
> Be cleansed and brightened and blessed!

[If you will charge and/or tune in this ritual as well, you can stop here, move onto the next step, and thank the spirits at the very end.]

With your pendulum cleansed, it is time to thank the elements:

> Spirits of Water, I thank you for your work.
> Spirits of Fire, I thank you for your work.
> Spirits of Air, I thank you for your work.

Spirits of Earth, I thank you for your work.

At the center I stood, and I stand there still.
All is as it was before, save the blessing.
I thank you all.

Now your pendulum is ready for charging.

A Simple Spirit Blessing for Charging

Place your pendulum onto the symbol of Spirit in the center, as you did for the cleansing. Here, we will call out to the spirits of the realms of Land, Sea, and Sky to bring their unique blessings to the pendulum and connect it to the rhythms of nature. Begin with this prayer to the Land Spirits:

I call out to the Spirits of Land:
You who know the ways of the forest,
Who hide in tree and field and under stone.
Bring forth the blessing of the Growing Green,
The cycle of life and death, birth and rebirth,
The joy of the folk in one another,
And the knowledge of turning seasons.
I honor you.

Now, call out in prayer to the Spirits of the Sea:

I call out to the Spirits of Sea:
You who ride the nine bright waves,
Who time the tide and sing sweet songs.
Bring forth the blessing of the Deep Waters,
The rhythm of lapping waves, of salty spray,
The plenty that sustains the folk,
And the knowledge of the deep still dark.
I honor you.

Now, call out in prayer to the Spirits of the Sky:

I call out to the Spirits of Sky:
You who glide in the highest heavens,
Who walk with broad steps in perfect time.
Bring forth the blessings of Cosmic Order,
The march of the sun, dance of the stars,
The wisdom of the moon that brings magic,
And the knowledge of the artful universe.
I honor you.

Now, with all the Spirits gathered, call out to them to charge your pendulum:

I call to all the Spirits here,
You I have honored, of Land, Sea, and Sky:
By all your Realms, may this tool be blessed.
May it know the rhythms of the world,
And may it never fail to reveal them.
So be it.

Take a moment to visualize the blessings flowing in: the light of the heavens shining down, the waters welling up, and the earth cradling the pendulum as it lays at the center of your altar. Know that it is good and ready.

[If you will tune in this ritual as well, you can stop here, move onto the next step, and thank the spirits at the very end.]

With your pendulum charged, it is time to thank the Spirits and the elements:

Spirits of all the Realms, I thank you for your work.
Spirits of Water, I thank you for your work.
Spirits of Fire, I thank you for your work.
Spirits of Air, I thank you for your work.
Spirits of Earth, I thank you for your work.

At the center I stood, and I stand there still.
All is as it was before, save the blessing.
I thank you all.

Now your pendulum is ready for tuning.

A Simple Tuning Tone

Place your pendulum in the center, upon the representation of Spirit, as you did for the cleansing and the charging. Now, we will attune this tool to your natural rhythms. This is done with a simple tone. Here are the instructions:

1. Begin by relaxing your body. Sit or stand straight, but not rigidly.
2. Focus on your intent: to provide your personal vibration and rhythm to the pendulum. You'll need to have this at the back of your mind as you prepare to start the toning.
3. Begin to breathe. Take at least three breaths (nine is a good number), paying attention to how you breathe each time. Feel each breath come in, and go out.
4. Once you have reached a point where your breath feels ready, begin to make a vocal tone. If you are not sure what it should sound like, try making some vowel sounds ("Ahhhhh," "Oooooo," and "Eeeeee" are very good ones to start with) or easy consonant sounds ("Mmmmmm" is very good for this). Let yourself settle into a sound that speaks to you, and direct it to the pendulum.

5. If you feel the energy of the tone flowing through you, you can direct it with your hands if you feel comfortable with that.

6. When you are ready, and you feel like the pendulum is in tune with your rhythms and vibrations, end the toning.

With your pendulum tuned, it is time to thank the Spirits and the elements:

Spirits of all the Realms, I thank you for your work.
Spirits of Water, I thank you for your work.
Spirits of Fire, I thank you for your work.
Spirits of Air, I thank you for your work.
Spirits of Earth, I thank you for your work.

At the center I stood, and I stand there still.
All is as it was before, save the blessing.
I thank you all.

Now your pendulum is ready for work. Enjoy it!

*G*ARANUS PUBLISHING

Pagan Fire Seminars
PFS1: From Private Practice to Public Ritual
Ritual Prep and Omen Journal

The Order Books of ADF
Volume 1: The Call of the Crane
Volume 2: The Order of Bardic Alchemy

The Guild Training Books of ADF
The Modern Day Warrior (First Circle Guide)

Books by Three Cranes Grove, ADF
The Fire on Our Hearth: a 3CG Devotional
The Crane Breviary and Guide Book
The ADF DP Through the Wheel of the Year
Sunna's Journey: Norse Liturgy for the Wheel of the Year
The Very Basics of Runes: Elder Futhark
3CG Membership Guide
Ritual Studies Journal

All available through The Magical Druid
magicaldruid.com
Columbus, OH